Beth's Yak

by Betty Sanford
illustrated by Shawn McManus

Core Decodable 59

Bothell, WA • Chicago, IL • Columbus, OH • New York, NY

MHEonline.com

Copyright © 2015 McGraw-Hill Education

All rights reserved. No part of this publication may be reproduced or distributed in any form or by any means, or stored in a database or retrieval system, without the prior written consent of McGraw-Hill Education, including, but not limited to, network storage or transmission, or broadcast for distance learning.

Send all inquiries to:
McGraw-Hill Education
8787 Orion Place
Columbus, OH 43240

ISBN: 978-0-02-145071-8
MHID: 0-02-145071-4

Printed in the United States of America.

2 3 4 5 6 7 8 9 DOC 20 19 18 17 16 15

Beth had a big yak.
Beth kept her yak with her.

Beth kept her yak on her bed.
Beth kept her yak in her yard.

Beth fed her yak yams. Yum!
The yak did not like grass. Yuck!

Beth has a yarn craft for her yak.

Beth sings to her yak.
Beth will not yell at her yak.

Is Beth's yak the best?
Beth thinks, "Yes!"